Adelaide Travel Guide

Sightseeing, Hotel, Restaurant & Shopping Highlights

Jack Burgess

Table of Contents

Adelaide

Named by Lonely Planet as one of its 'Top 10 Must-Visit Cities of 2014', the city of Adelaide is an emerging international tourist destination in South Australia. Adelaide has also been ranked as the most liveable city in Australia and as one of the 'Top 10 Most Liveable Cities in the World' by The Economist.

From the rolling Adelaide Hills to the stunning beaches, from the heritage-listed buildings to the wide streets lined with skyscrapers, Adelaide encapsulates a complete experience for every visitor.

Located on the south east coast of Australia, Adelaide is the capital of the state of South Australia and is one of the major cities in the country. Founded in 1836, the city was the planned capital for the British province in Australia. It was intended for free settlers and was never a convict settlement like the other major Australian cities. It was named after Princess Adelaide of Saxe-Meiningen, Queen Consort to King William IV. Once called the City Of Churches for the religious freedom and civil liberties.

Cradled amidst some of the best wine regions of the country (Adelaide was the first Australian city to export wine in 1845), Adelaide is set in a systematic grid layout interspaced by public squares and parklands. There are plenty of attractions in and around the city. From the airport and the hills to the beautiful beaches, everything is just a short drive away, earning the city the moniker – The 20-minute City! It is also a popular festival city in the country with numerous annual festivals, exhibitions, and events keeping the cultural calendar chock-a-block.

A trip to Adelaide is unlike visiting any other city. The genuine warmth of the Adelaideans makes one feel welcome from the very onset. The city has many historic, scenic, and natural landmarks which are a delight to pick from during the vacation. Neighbouring attractions like the Kangaroo Island and the McVale Wine Region are great for a day trip with the whole family. One is certainly spoilt for choice in this city with such a variety of offerings. As is correctly said about Adelaide – it is waiting to be uncorked and sampled!

Culture

Being a Commonwealth city, Adelaide has had a strong British influence from its founding days. In the decades that followed, because of the liberal religious following of the city, immigrants from other European countries settled in, especially the religious non-conformists.

Post World War II saw a major influx of European immigrants followed by the Indo-Chinese in the 1970s. This diversity in ethnicity, from the Aboriginal history to the post-War migration, helped shape a unique mix of events and festivals in the city.

Even the religious monuments like the Adelaide Mosque (Little Gilbert Street), or the St Peter's Cathedral (Pennington Terrace) and the West Terrace Cemetery are an architectural delight. Festivals like the Italian Carnevale, Greek Glendi, or the German Schutzenfest bring different parts of the world under the Adelaidean sky.

There are a number of Aboriginal attractions in Adelaide. The Tandanya is the oldest Aboriginal owned multi-arts centre in the country. Free entry and free tours are available at this centre that not only displays Aboriginal art, but also hosts musical performances every week. Plaques, memorials, and artwork dedicated to the Aboriginal people can be seen at Elder Park, Adelaide Festival Centre, and Piltawodli Park.

Adelaide has many festivals throughout the year, especially in March – known as Mad March for the number of festivities. Adelaide Festival, WOMADelaide, Adelaide Casino Cup, Adelaide Cabaret Festival, and Adelaide Film Festival are just some of the events that are held in March. The winter months that follow celebrate the Come Out Festival, the LGBT Feast Festival, and the Adelaide International Guitar Festival. The Adelaide Christmas pageant, staged in early November is the largest of its kind in the world, and is attended by near half a million people.

Music lovers can choose from the formal classical opera performances to the youthful and wild pop concerts. The Town Hall and the Elder Hall hosts performances by the Adelaide Symphony Orchestra and the Adelaide Youth Orchestra. Popular concert venues include the Apollo Stadium, Adelaide Entertainment Centre, and the Adelaide Oval.

There is a lot to cheer for art lovers. Along with public art exhibits, the city has a number of art galleries including the Art Gallery of SA, BMG Art, Nexus, and the Australian Experimental Art Foundation.

Location & Orientation

Located to the north of the Fleurieu Peninsula, Adelaide is a coastal city on the Gulf of St Vincent. The closest major cities are Melbourne (653 km) and Canberra (958 km). It is served by the Adelaide International Airport (IATA: ADL) - http://www.adelaideairport.com.au/. Located about 7 km west of the Adelaide city centre, this busy airport caters to over 7 million passengers annually connecting the city to its Australian neighbours and many other cities worldwide. The airport is ranked as the 2nd best airport in the world in the 5-15 million passengers category.

There are multiple modes of transport from the airport to the city and the suburbs. The Adelaide Airport Flyer – http://www.adelaideairportflyer.com/ operates door-to-door minibus shuttles.

The public bus service, by JetBus, has connections (J1 and J2) that run every 15 minutes for the 20-miniute commute to the city centre. Single-trip ticket costs $5 (Australian dollar). Skylink Shuttle connects the airport, Keswick Interstate Rail Terminal, and the city and costs $10 ($4 to the train terminal) for the one-way trip. Taxis are readily available and are the quickest mode of transport and are often a better choice than the shuttle if there are 2 or 3 passengers. Fare to the city centre costs approximately $15; there is an extra $2 levy for all airport pickups. Rental car desks are located at the ground level and one can choose from any of the major brands including Hertz, Europcar, Avis, and Budget.

The Great Southern Railway -
http://www.greatsouthernrail.com.au connects Adelaide
by rail to the other Australian cities. Due to the long
distances between the major Australian cities, many of the
train journeys in this country are quite long but not
necessarily tedious because of the stunning landscape.
The Ghan connecting Adelaide to Darwin, and the India
Pacific, connecting the city to Perth and Sydney are
considered 2 of the greatest train journeys in the world.
Fares are certainly not cheap for this lifetime experience.
One-way trip from Adelaide to Darwin on The Ghan can
cost from $647 (day-night seat) to $6000 (premium Gold
cabin for 2 guests), whereas an Adelaide-Sydney one-way
trip on the India Pacific ranges from $375 to $2400! Such is
the luxury of these train rides that one can even take the
car on the train!

For those opting for a cheaper alternative can choose the
bus. Greyhound Australia-
http://www.greyhound.com.au/ has multiple
connections to the city and offers many packages as well
as hop-on-hop-off passes.

Once in the city, one can use the free CityLoop buses.
These buses run in a clockwise and anti-clockwise
direction and connect most of the major attractions (Bus
No. 99C covers a number of tourist attractions). Service is
reduced after 6:00 pm and stops at midnight.

The Adelaide Metro - http://www.adelaidemetro.com.au/ is the official operator for the city tram, bus, and subway. A single trip costs $4.90 so it is always better to buy a day ticket for $9.10 for unlimited travel. Tickets can be bought on board or from corner stores and vending machines at different locations in the city. Visitors can also use the Shuttle Tram – a free service between South Terrace and North Terrace. Adelaide is also home to the Tindo – the first solar-powered bus in the world. Again a free service, the Tindo travels between North Adelaide and the city centre.

For those opting for a private vehicle, taxis are available just a call away at Access Cabs (Tel: 1300 360 940) and Suburban Taxis (Tel: 13 10 08). Rental cars are offered by all major brands. For those planning to drive, it has to be kept in mind that Australia has a left-lane driving rule. Speed limits are 110 km per hr for highways and 50 km per hr for built-up areas. Speed limits are strictly enforced and driving even 5 km above the speed limit will incur a fine. To drive in Australia, one must be 21 years of age and have an International Driver's License in English.

Cycling enthusiasts can pick a free bicycle from any of the 3 Adelaide City Bike depots near the city centre. Protective gear and a lock are given as add-on benefits. With flat streets and a visitor-friendly layout in and around the city, cycling and walking are very reasonable options to see this city.

Climate & When to Visit

Adelaide experiences a warm Mediterranean climate with mild and wet winters and warm drier summers. Being in the southern hemisphere, Adelaide has its winter between May and October when the Celsius averages a high of 17 degrees and reaches a low of around 7 degrees. June is often the coldest and the wettest month of the year. Summer months, between November and April have an average high of around 28 degrees Celsius and an average low of around 17 degrees Celsius. Due to the warm and dry weather, the Adelaide summer is the perfect time to visit the city. Many festivals and public events are also scheduled during this time of the year

Sightseeing Highlights

Adelaide Hills

Part of the Mount Lofty Ranges, the Adelaide Hills are on the east of the city of Adelaide stretching from Barossa in the north to the Kuitpo Forest in the south. It is located about a 30-minite drive from the Adelaide CBD. It can be easily reached by bus - http://www.transitplus.com.au - from the central bus station on Franklin Street. For those preferring to drive, it is recommended to download a map as there is poor signage on the hills.

Once on the Adelaide Hills, there are a number of attractions to choose from.

Mt Lofty

The highest point of the hills is the Mt Lofty at 712m above sea level. The Mt Lofty Lookout - http://www.mtloftysummit.com/ is a must-visit place on the hills with stunning panoramic views of the city and the Gulf of St Vincent. The restaurant and the café at the lookout is the ideal place for a drink or a romantic dinner with the sunset as the backdrop. Reservations are strongly recommended for those who are planning a dinner at the restaurant. There is also a plaza where many private and public events are hosted.

Botanic Gardens of Adelaide – Mt Lofty

Located on the hills with stunning views, the Botanic Garden (Tel: 08 8370 8370) has collections from various parts of the world including South America, North America, East Africa, New Zealand, China, and South East Asia. Spanning over 100 hectares, it has an expansive bushland, artistic sculptures, and many walking and hiking trails. It is open from 8:30 am to 4:00 pm on weekdays and from 10:00 am to 5:00 pm on weekends, but may remain closed if there is any prediction of fire danger. Admission is free.

Hahndorf

The small town of Hahndorf is the oldest surviving German settlement in Australia. A centre for farming in the past, the town is currently dependant on the tourism industry.

The German influence and heritage is still retained in Hahndorf as one can see many German bakeries and goods outlets. In fact, one will find many boutique cellars on the main street, giving a very European feel to the town. Walking along the main street, one is also greeted by century old elm trees and beautifully restored buildings.

Two of the religious attractions in town are the 1839 St Michael's Lutheran Church - the oldest Lutheran church in Australia; and the 1846 St Lutheran Church. The cold-climate of the town is ideal for winemaking and there are many opportunities to try the local wine which has made a name for itself in the global market. If visiting during the season, one can also get some the best strawberries in the country.

Hahndorf is home to many landscape artists and artisans and it is no wonder that there are many souvenir and gift shops where one can pick some unique gifts to make the visit memorable. The Hahndorf Academy - http://www.hahndorfacademy.org.au/ is one such place where local arts and crafts are highlighted and promoted. It also has a museum on German migration and German art.

Although Hahndorf retains an old European charm, it is also recognized as a trendy place for a romantic getaway or a quiet day-off. Many chic restaurants and cafes offer the very best in the world of cuisine.

National Motor Museum

Since its founding in 1965 in Birdwood, the National Motor Museum has greeted millions of enthusiasts with its collection, display and education of Australian transport over the centuries. With over 300 vehicles on display, it is the largest motor museum in Australia.

The collections at the museum range from vintage and classic vehicles to modern vehicles and motorcycles. There is also a section on toys and models.

The museum is open daily (except Dec 25) from 10:00 am to 5:00 pm. Ticket prices are: Adult - $12; and Child - $5. Concession tickets and group discounts are available.

Glenelg

With spectacular sandy beaches, al fresco dining, 200 specialty shops, heritage walks, and a vibrant nightlife, the beach suburb of Glenelg is a popular destination for the locals and tourists alike. Located on the Holdfast Bay shore, Glenelg was founded in 1836, making it the oldest European settlement in the Australian mainland.

Glenelg is conveniently connected to Adelaide by the Anzac Highway. One can use the Adelaide Metro service to reach Glenelg. It is interesting to note that the only tram that operates in the city of Adelaide is the Glenelg Tram - a route that was established in 1873 and is still operational. The highlight is the early 19th century tram that is used on this route on weekends and holidays. Once in Glenelg, most of the attractions can be seen on foot, especially on Jetty Road, the main street that cuts through the middle of the town.

A walk through the streets is nothing short of a heritage walk and one is easily transported back by decades. History lovers can head to the Bay Discovery Centre in the Glenelg Town Hall. The Centre - a museum of social history highlighting the cultural heritage of the region has numerous displays of paintings, sculptures, photographs, jewelry, and other forms of artworks by established as well as rising Australian artists. This self-guided museum is open from 10:00 am to 5:00 pm every day and has free entry.

The Glenelg seafront is packed with activities throughout the week, and gets especially busy on the weekends. Other than just relaxing on the beach, one can engage in many beach activities like scuba diving and beach volleyball. Dolphin watching is also very popular. The multi-award winning Temptation Sailing (Tel: 412 811 838) takes its guests on a 58ft catamaran for a guaranteed full-commentary dolphin cruise. There are a lot of fun activities for families with kids. The Ice Arena, Laser Skirmish, Plaster Fun House, The Fairy Bay Shop, and the Treasure Hunt can keep any kid happy for hours. There is also the refurbished 120-year old carousel, mini golf, and waterslides for the whole family to enjoy.

Glenelg has a very vibrant nightlife with many restaurants, bars, cafes, and nightclubs. There are a wide range of exquisite restaurants for fine dining on Jetty Road, Henley Beach, and Brighton. The Pier Bar, The Grand Bar, Broadway Hotel, and the Jetty Hotel are the popular nightlife spots in town.

Glenelg is also a haven for shopaholics. Harbor Town – about 10 minutes from town – has numerous shopping outlets where one can hunt for great deals. Souvenir stores can be found on Jetty Road, Sussex Street, and the Marina Pier.

McLaren Vale Wine Region

Located about 35 km south of Adelaide and ideal for a day trip, the McLaren Vale Wine Region is regarded as the birthplace of the wine industry of South Australia and is home to some of the oldest grape vines in the world. The region has about 65 boutique-sized wineries with nearly 300 independent grape growers.

The McLaren Vale Wine Region is between the Mt Lofty range of hills and the Gulf of St Vincent beaches. Known for its dry Mediterranean-styled climate, the region was originally used for growing cereal crops. Grape vines were planted in the 1st quarter of the 19th century and the region has been known for the wineries ever since. Different types of wines are produced here but the most popular is the Shiraz. Other major varieties from the region include Cabernet Sauvignon, Grenache, and Chardonnay.

Such is the popularity and influence of wine making in the McLaren Vale Township that many of the roads are named after famous wine making families of the region. There are many interesting wine trails in and around McLaren Vale including the Coast to Vines Rail Trail, Shiraz Trail, and the Kidman Trail. Fresh produce does not begin and end with grape growing in the region. The weekend farmer's market is a great place to buy some of the tastiest cheese and locally harvested olives.

On a sunny day one can also head to the Onkaparinge River to paddle a canoe. The river, the 2nd longest of the island nation, leads into the Onkaparinge National Park which has the Echidna Trail with ruins and heritage-listed huts from the late 19th century. Adventure and nature lovers can also head to the Fleurieu Peninsula to observe the rich wildlife or engage in diving and fishing.

Port Adelaide

Located about 14 km northwest of the Adelaide city centre, Port Adelaide is the main port of the city and a part of the City of Port Adelaide Enfield. Gateway for Adelaide to the rest of the world, Port Adelaide was established in the mid 19th century and has played a major role in the shaping the growth of the city. The area is known as the history precinct for the presence of a number of museums and numerous 19th century pubs and buildings.

Popular historical sites in the Port area include the Port Hotel that was opened in 1838. The British Hotel which opened in 1947 is credited for being the longest continually licensed hotel in the area. The late Victorian-styled Dockside Tavern, The Golden Port Tavern, and the Port Dock Brewery Hotel are all operational for over a 100 years and are tourist attractions for their colonial architectural style and of course, their age. A walk along the docks will also take one past some of the finest and oldest colonial buildings in the country. One can also book a cruise at the Port for dolphin watching. For the fitness enthusiasts, kayaking is an option to explore in the Port area.

The 8 km of clean sand from the North Haven to Sephamore is dotted with many restaurants, cafes, and souvenir stores. The Windsor Gardens and Regency Park are not simply public parks, but hubs for public art and cultural heritage. While the adventure lovers can head for kart racing, rock climbing, or laser skirmish; history lovers can head to one of the many museums in Port Adelaide.

Museums in the Port area include the Enfield Heritage Museum (Regency Park), National Railway Museum (Lipson Street), South Australian Aviation Museum (South Lipson Street), Port Adelaide Maritime Museum (Fletcher Road), and South Australian Maritime Museum (Lipson Street). Art lovers can choose from one of the many galleries in town. Café shops and specialty stores also host exhibitions from time to time. Popular galleries include the Sephamore Angel, Mark Lobert Gallery, and Better World Arts. Many of the regular galleries are located on Lipson Street, Port Road, and Commercial Road.

A popular family event in the Port calendar is the Port Festival (usually in October). With free entry to the museums, food stalls, exhibitions, free guided tours, screenings, artists' market, performances, and fun activities for the whole family, the Port area is transformed into a fun arena for a weekend every year.

Kangaroo Island

The 3rd largest Australian island, Kangaroo Island, is also the largest sand island in the world. With pristine wilderness where one can see pelicans flying across the blue skies or koalas cuddling against the eucalyptus trees, no wonder it is one of the most visited tourist attractions in Australia. Iconic Australian landscape and endemic wildlife of the country make the island a top draw for the tourists.

Kangaroo Island is linked by air and sea from the Australian mainland. Rex Airlines - http://www.rex.com.au/ operates daily flights (approx 30 min) from the Adelaide Airport. Ferry services (45min) are available from Cape Jervis – about a 2 km drive from Adelaide CBD. There are coach connections from Adelaide CBD to the ferry port.

Once on the island, one can enjoy sighting many Australian birds and animals that are protected in a natural environment through many nature reserves and national parks. One of the most popular is the Flinders Chase National Park near the south coast of the island. Home to endangered species like the koala, platypus, fur seals, goannas, and echidnas; the Park is also known for many natural wonders like the Admirals Arch and the iconic Remarkable Rocks.

The island has a number of wildlife attractions and tours including the Hanson Bay Wildlife Sanctuary Tour (includes koala sightings and the famous nocturnal tour), Kangaroo Island Penguin Centre Tour (includes an aquarium visit, penguin colony visit, and feeding the fish and pelicans), and Penneshaw Penguin Centre Tour (nocturnal tour of penguin colony).

The island has many trails and walks for visitors of different fitness levels. Whereas the Ironstone Hill Hike, Fish Cannery Walk, Kingscote Coastal Walk, and Murray Lagoon Walk explore the coast and marine life on the island, the Clifftop Hike, Weirs Cove Hike, and the Cape du Couedic Hike explore the scenic beauty with panoramic views of the island and its surroundings.

Kangaroo Island has a range of accommodations for those who want to stay overnight (especially for the nocturnal tours). There are also many facilities for dining. The island also has great opportunities for shopping, especially lavender products and mosaic-glass artworks.

North Terrace

Running east to west, the North Terrace links the Adelaide CBD to the residential suburbs of the city. A stroll along the North Terrace takes one past a number of public buildings, state offices, and attractions. It is one of the most beautiful and decorated parts of the city.

The National Wine Centre on Hackney Road - http://www.wineaustralia.com.au/ is not only a great place to learn about wine making in this part of the country but also to taste some of the products of the region. One can also enjoy a great meal from the tapas menu of the Cellar Door eatery.

King William Road has the Old Parliament House of South Australia - http://www.parliament.sa.gov.au. The Old Parliament House that took 65 years to complete in 1939 is a grand building with Corinthian columns. Although the original plan had a dome and towers, the final execution was devoid of any extravagance due to financial constraints.

The 1856 Adelaide Railway Station is located near the Morphett Street Bridge. The building also houses the Adelaide Casino in a section that is not used by the railway. This terminal station handles over 40000 passengers every day. The station, which was rebuilt in the mid 1980s, includes some heritage-listed sections.

Kintore Avenue is home to the State Library of South Australia - http://www.slsa.sa.gov.au, the mid 19th century South Australian Museum of Natural History, and the 1881 Art Gallery of South Australia. The avenue is also home to the main campuses of the University of Adelaide and the University of South Australia.

The southern part of the North Terrace also has a number of attractions. The Anglican Holy Trinity Church is the largest Anglican Church in the province of South Australia. It also has the historic Scots Church, and the Christian Scientist Church (Pulteney Street).

Other than some parks and parklands, North Terrace has some shopping centres including the popular Myers House and the Rundle Mall.

St Francis Xavier Cathedral

Affiliated to Roman Catholicism, the St Francis Xavier Cathedral is housed in a Gothic Revival styled building. Although the ground breaking was done in 1856 and the first consecration was done 2 years later, the Cathedral was completed in as late as 1996!

The dominating church building has a 36m high tower and has a length of 56.5m. The statue of St John the Baptist on the north western corner of the church was carved in 1925 in Tuscany. The other end - south west corner - has The Lady Altar carved from Carrara marble with inset panels made from the lapis stone. The western side of the Cathedral has the bronze statues of Jesus and Joseph. The eastern side of the Cathedral has the statue of St Patrick. The southern end - the front façade - of the church has lancet windows with beautiful religious artwork.

The cathedral stays busy with Mass, confessions, funerals, weddings, and many other religious festivals. Not only can one visit the church between 7:30 am and 6:30 pm on any day, one can also book a guided tour at http://www.adelcathparish.org/Ministries/Friends-of-Cathedral.htm.

Belair National Park

Located 13 km south of Adelaide, Belair National Park (Tel: 08 8278 5477) is the place to be for those who are looking for some outdoor activities. Established in 1891, the Park is the oldest national park in the state and the 2nd oldest in the country. The park spans 835ha and has ample opportunities for recreational and social activities set in an outdoor environment. The Park attracts over a quarter million visitors every year.

The region, one of the few biodiversity hotspots in the country, provides an undisturbed environment for wildlife to flourish - both in the form of flora and fauna. Upgraded with picnic spots and other visitor facilities, the Park is a great place to go for a hike, soak in nature, or to enjoy a fun day out with the whole family. The Park has many facilities for playing tennis, weddings, and for group events. Popular trails in the Park include the Wood Duck Dawdle, Valley Loop Walk, Waterfall Hike, and the Lorikeet Loop Walk.

Public transport to the Park is available from the Adelaide CBD. It is open from 8:00 am until sunset every day, except Christmas Day. The Park may remain closed if there are fire predictions or warnings. There are specific rates for entry and using the park facilities, details of which may be found at: http://www.environment.sa.gov.au/parks/Find_a_Park/Browse_by_region/Adelaide_Hills/Belair_National_Park/Fees.

Migration Museum

82 Kintore Avenue
Adelaide SA
Tel: 08 8207 7580
http://migration.historysa.com.au/

Established in 1986, the unique Migration Museum is involved with the migration and settlement history of the state of South Australia.

The oldest of its kind in the country, the Migration Museum aims at promoting multiculturalism and cultural diversity and addresses the different aspects of ethnicity, gender, class, region, and age. The museum is a great place to discover the identities of various communities and cultures of South Australia.

The museum has a number of permanent and floating exhibitions. The permanent exhibitions include Impact - a pictorial depiction illustrating the impact of migration on the lives and culture of the Aboriginal people. Behind the Wall is a poignant depiction of the lives - and death - of poor and homeless women and children who lived in the Destitute Asylum. 'Strangers in a Strange Land' tells the stories of the immigrants to South Australia in the late 19th century. 'Leaving Britain and Establishing South Australia' is another interesting permanent exhibition that looks into the lives of the British who moved here to establish a British colony. 'Immigration in the Twentieth Century' and 'Into the Twenty First Century' are 2 other permanent exhibitions that not only look into the stories of immigration of the said centuries but also into, how Australia was able to embrace multiculturalism and develop a diverse cultural scene.

Located close to the Rundle Mall, the Museum is open from 10:00 am to 5:00 pm on weekdays and from 1:00 pm to 5:00 pm on weekends and public holidays. It is closed on Christmas Day and Good Friday. Admission is free.

Adelaide Zoo

Frome Road
Adelaide SA 5000
Tel: 08 8267 3255
http://www.zoossa.com.au/adelaide-zoo

Located north of the Adelaide city centre, the Adelaide Zoo is the 2nd oldest zoo in the country and the only one that is a non-profit organization. Spread over 20 acres, the zoo has over 2000 animals from 300 different species. The premise of the zoo itself is of architectural interest and some parts of it are listed as heritage site.

Having opened in 1883, the zoo today is the home to many animals and birds, some endemic to Australia. The zoo enclosure has birds like finches, parrots, and flamingoes. The zoo originally had 10 flamingoes but many of those were killed in a 1915 drought - today only 2 flamingoes over 70 years of age are the prized possession of the zoo. The zoo has animals from different regions. Animals from the Asian region include the Sumatran Tiger, Sacred Kingfisher, Emerald Dove, Giant Panda, Red Panda, and the Mandarin Duck. From the African region there is the African Lion, Cheetah, Ostrich, Giraffe, and Hamadryas Baboon, to name a few. South America is represented by the Brazilian Tapir, Blue and Gold Macaw, Galapagos Tortoise, and the Chilean Flamingo. Of course, there are many Australian birds and animals including the Australian Fur Seal, Red Kangaroo, and Freckled Duck. The zoo arranges a number of encounters (with the birds and animals) and tours for the visiting guests, details of which are posted on the website.

The zoo is open 9:30 am to 5:00 pm everyday and has an entry fee $31.50 for age 15 years and above. Group and family discounts are available.

Recommendations for the Budget Traveller

Places to Stay

Mantra Hindmarsh Square

55 -67 Hindmarsh Square
Adelaide SA 5000
Tel: 08 8412 3333
http://www.mantra.com.au

Located just minutes away from the Adelaide Convention Centre and the Adelaide Cricket Ground in the CBD, the Mantra Hindmarsh Square offers a combination of convenience with style.

Facilities include a 24-hour reception, 24-hr room service, undercover parking (for a fee), travel desk, and laundry facilities. There is free Wi-Fi in the premise. The hotel has a restaurant, lounge bar, and gymnasium.

The apartment-styled rooms come with a kitchenette and some even have a balcony. Room rates start from $129.

Adelaide Royal Coach

24 Dequetteville Terrace
Adelaide SA 5067
Tel: 08 8362 5676
http://www.royalcoach.com.au/

Located close to the business district, the Adelaide Royal Coach is a 3-storey motel with a 90s décor. The National Wine Centre and the East End Precinct are attractions near the motel. There is a 24-hr reception, free parking, and free Wi-Fi. There is a swimming pool, bar, and a restaurant in the premises. Non-smoking rooms and breakfast in the rooms are available.

There are a variety of rooms from the general double rooms to the spa suite. Room rates start from $100.

Adelaide City Park Motel

471 Pulteney Street
Adelaide SA
Tel: 08 8223 1444
http://www.citypark.com.au/

This boutique motel with exquisitely detailed interiors is located at the heart of the city centre, offering a tranquil retreat at affordable rates. Leather lounges and French prints create a warm décor for this motel. This non-smoking property has free parking and Wi-Fi. There is a travel desk and arrangement for airport pick-ups and drops.

Rooms have ensuite bathrooms and tea and coffee facilities. Room rates start from $80 if booked online in advance.

Glenelg Motel

41 Tapleys Hill Road
Glenelg, SA 5045
Tel: 08 8295 7141
http://www.glenelgmotel.com.au

Located just a 5-minute walk from the beach, the Glenelg Motel comes with free parking, free Wi-Fi, and a travel desk. Non-smoking and family rooms are available as well as facilities for disabled guests. There is an outdoor pool and barbeque area. The reception desk closes at 9:00 pm so guests coming after 9:00 pm should notify the motel for late check-in.

Rooms come with ensuite bathroom, LCD TV, tea and coffee facilities, and hairdryer. Room rates start from $110.

The Hotel Metropolitan

46 Grote Street
Adelaide SA 5000
Tel: 08 8231 5471
http://www.hotelmetro.com.au/

The Hotel Metropolitan is housed in a heritage-listed building that was built in 1883.

It is located right at the heart of the city centre adjacent to the Her Majesty's Theatre and the Adelaide Central Markets. The hotel has been functional as a pub from the very beginning and still offers the same, along with games and entertainment. There is free parking and Wi-Fi. Family and non-smoking rooms are available. There is an onsite ATM machine.

Rooms come with a balcony and range from single to multi-person. Room rates start from $55.

Places to Eat

Georges on Waymouth

20 Waymouth Street
Adelaide SA 5000
Tel: 08 8211 6960
http://www.georgesonwaymouth.com.au/

Located in the heart of the Adelaide CBD, the Georges on Waymouth is a multi-award winning restaurant serving Mediterranean cuisine in a European setting. Food is cooked with freshly available produce and the menu for the season is set accordingly. Vegetarian starters are priced about $18. Hand-made pasta is priced between $30-35. Main dishes of pork, beef, or meat are priced between $35 and $40. Dessert wine is offered – priced around $75(circa 2009) for 375ml.

Auge Ristorante

22 Grote Street
Adelaide SA 5000
Tel: 08 8410 9332
http://www.auge.com.au/

As is obvious from the name, this restaurant serves Italian cuisine and is a favorite for business lunches as well as for special occasion dining, at an affordable price. A well-trained attentive staff with excellent service adds to the reputation. Both vegetarian and non-vegetarian entrees are priced at $24. Main dishes of duck, pork, or fish are priced at $39. Italian desserts are priced at $16.50. The restaurant accepts all major credit cards as well as bitcoins.

Taste of Nepal

300 The Parade
Adelaide SA 5068
Tel: 08 8332 2788
http://www.tasteofnepal.com.au/

Serving Nepalese and Indian cuisine, the Taste of Nepal is a favorite with diners, local and visitors alike. If informed earlier, the restaurant makes an effort to cook to accommodate guests with specific food-allergies or any special request.

Entrees (momos and fried vegetables) are priced at $10.50. Main dishes (grilled meat, various non-vegetarian curries) are priced between $20 and $26. Vegan and vegetarian dishes are priced between $17 and $22. It also offers a wide variety of wines.

Jolleys Boathouse Restaurant

1 Jolleys Lane
Adelaide SA 5000
Tel: 08 8223 2891
http://www.jolleysboathouse.com/

Serving international and Australian cuisine, the restaurant serves all the major meals of the day, from breakfast and lunch, to late night dinner. The menu is seasonal depending on the best available produce in the market. Entrees (seafood, chicken, and vegetarian) are priced around $20. Main dishes (of lamb, chicken, and beef) are priced around $35. There is also a huge variety of beer, champagne, and wine to choose from.

Vietnam Restaurant

73 Addison Road
Adelaide SA 5013
Tel: 08 8447 3395
http://www.vietnamrestaurant.com.au/

Established almost 3 decades ago, this is one of the oldest Vietnamese restaurants in Adelaide. This multi award winning restaurant is one of the best places to try Asian cuisine. One can try authentic Vietnamese dishes like the Hot and Sour Fish Soup ($40 – to share), Barbeque quails ($30), Rice paper rolls with stuffing ($4.40), and Crispy king prawns in ginger and chilli ($30). Set menus are also available for groups. Reservations are recommended for this busy restaurant.

Places to Shop

Rundle Mall

Located on Pulteney Street and Rundle Street, the Rundle Mall is the first pedestrian mall in Australia – after traffic was closed on the Rundle Street on September 1976. The mall retains its place as one of the premiere shopping destinations in the city with over a 1000 stores that include many flagship stores along with small independent retailers. It has multiple food courts, bars, and restaurants. The Rundle Mall precinct is also home to over half a dozen places of accommodation! It is a perfect place to not only shop till you drop, but also grab a bite or retire for the day.

North Adelaide Village

http://www.northadelaidevillage.com.au

Located in the famed North Adelaide suburb with numerous restaurants, bars, and shopping centres, the North Adelaide Village is a one stop shopping centre with a variety of stores that include bookstores, salon, jewelry store, optometrist, gym, and a gourmet supermarket. This is the place if someone is looking for cutting edge fashion. The centre also has many restaurants and banks. It is open from 9:00 am to around 5:30 pm with extended hours (9:00pm) on Thursdays.

Adelaide Central Market

Located near the corner of Grote Street, this central market is popular for the fresh produce. This 140 year old market is one of the oldest indoor markets in the world and is a major tourist attraction. It is often called the 'Heart of Adelaide'. Adelaide and its surroundings have a very favourable climate for some Mediterranean-type vegetation and this is the market where one can buy the produce. The market is open from Tuesday to Saturday.

Skye Cellars

578 The Parade
Adelaide SA 5072
Tel: 08 8332 6407
http://www.skyecellars.com.au

Housed in the heritage-listed Auldana Estate Winery, this is a place where one can get some great bargains for the famous South Australian wines. It is 15 minutes from the Adelaide CBD and the ideal place to pick a bottle of wine if one is running a tight schedule and cannot visit the wine region. They have excellently trained staff who may even offer a wine tasting session before recommending a variety.

Gepps Cross Treasure Market

Gepps Cross
Adelaide SA 5094
Tel: 08 8352 1377
http://www.wallis.com.au/gepps-x-market

The biggest outdoor market in the state is also the perfect place to hunt for bargains. From the freshest of fruits and vegetables to the wide variety of antiques and secondhand items, this flea market has something for everyone. It is open every Sunday morning and buyers are allowed from 7:00 am. It is a good idea to get there early to get the best bargains as well as to avoid the crowd.

Printed in Great Britain
by Amazon.co.uk, Ltd.,
Marston Gate.